Write the letter that begins each picture's name by its picture.
Follow the **b** words to help the bird get to her nest.

a b c d e f g h i j k l m n o p q r s t u v w x y z

Alphabet Fun!

FUN WITH THE LETTERS D, E & F

Practice tracing and writing each letter.

Beginning Sounds
Write the letters that begin the picture words.

_____ og

_____ gg

_____ an

Tic-Tac-Toe
Draw a line through the pictures that start with the same letter.

A B C D E F G H I J K L M N O P Q R S T U V W X Y Z

How Many?

Find the pictures that start with the letters **d**, **e**, and **f**.

Letter Match

Draw lines from the uppercase letters to the matching lowercase letters.

D

E

F

f

e

d

Beginning Sounds

Say the picture words. Circle the letters that begin the picture words.

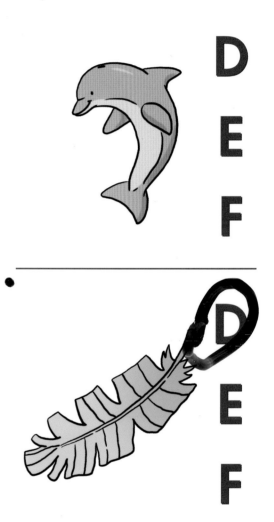

D
E
F

D
E
F

D
E
F

Alphabet Fun!

FUN WITH THE LETTERS G, H & I

Practice tracing and writing each letter.

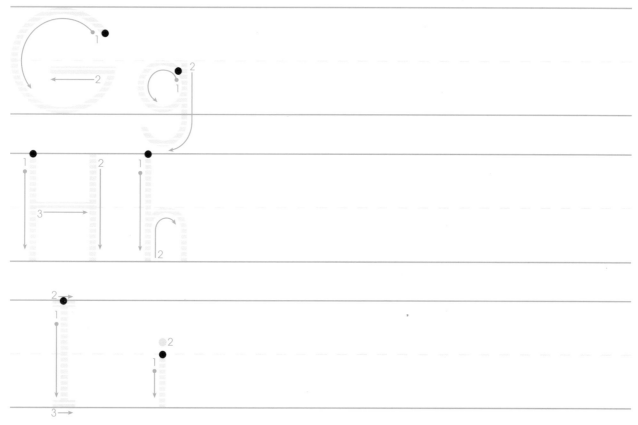

Beginning Sounds

Write the letters that begin the picture words.

_____ irl

_____ at

_____ nsects

Tic-Tac-Toe

Draw a line through the pictures that start with the same letter.

A B C D E F G H I J K L M N O P Q R S T U V W X Y Z

How Many?

Find the pictures that start with the letters **g**, **h**, and **i**.

Letter Match

Draw lines from the uppercase letters to the matching lowercase letters.

G   i

H   h

I   g

Beginning Sounds

Say the picture words. Circle the letters that begin the picture words.

G H I

G H I

G H I

a b c d e f **g h i** j k l m n o p q r s t u v w x y z

Practice tracing and writing each letter.

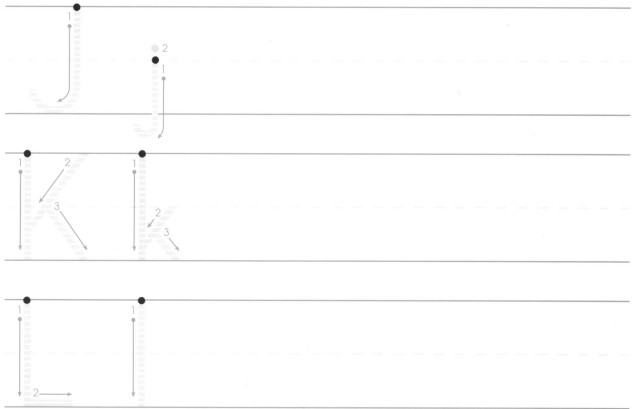

Beginning Sounds

Write the letters that begin the picture words.

_____ et

_____ ey

_____ amp

Tic-Tac-Toe

Draw a line through the pictures that start with the same letter.

A B C D E F G H I J K L M N O P Q R S T U V W X Y Z

How Many?

Find the pictures that start with the letters **j**, **k**, and **l**.

Beginning Sounds

Say the picture words. Circle the letters that begin the picture words.

J
K
L

J
K
L

J
K
L

Letter Match

Draw lines from the uppercase letters to the matching lowercase letters.

J

K

L

j

k

l

FUN WITH THE LETTERS M, N & O

Practice tracing and writing each letter.

Beginning Sounds

Write the letters that begin the picture words.

_____ ouse

_____ est

_____ x

Tic-Tac-Toe

Draw a line through the pictures that start with the same letter.

A B C D E F G H I J K L M N O P Q R S T U V W X Y Z

How Many?

Find the pictures that start with the letters **m**, **n**, and **o**.

Beginning Sounds

Say the picture words. Circle the letters that begin the picture words.

M N O

M N O

M N O

Letter Match

Draw lines from the uppercase letters to the matching lowercase letters.

M   n

N   o

O   m

a b c d e f g h i j k l m n o p q r s t u v w x y z

Alphabet Fun!

FUN WITH THE LETTERS P, Q & R

Practice tracing and writing each letter.

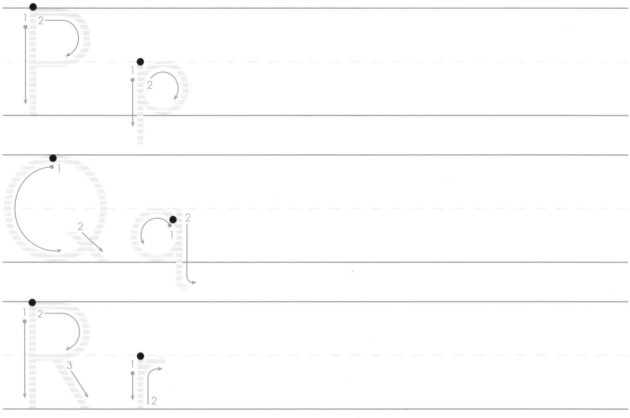

Beginning Sounds

Write the letters that begin the picture words.

_____ ig

_____ ueen

_____ ing

Tic-Tac-Toe

Draw a line through the pictures that start with the same letter.

A B C D E F G H I J K L M N O P Q R S T U V W X Y Z

How Many?

Find the pictures that start with the letters **p**, **q**, and **r**.

Beginning Sounds

Say the picture words. Circle the letters that begin the picture words.

P
Q
R

P
Q
R

P
Q
R

Letter Match

Draw lines from the uppercase letters to the matching lowercase letters.

P

Q

R

r

q

p

a b c d e f g h i j k l m n o p q r s t u v w x y z

Alphabet Fun!

FUN WITH THE LETTERS S, T & U

Practice tracing and writing each letter.

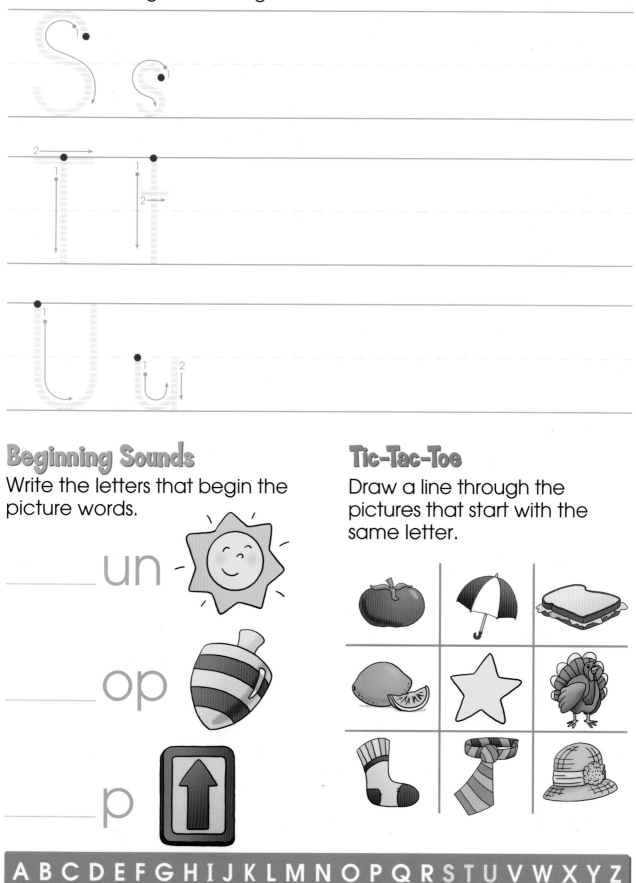

Beginning Sounds

Write the letters that begin the picture words.

_____ un

_____ op

_____ p

Tic-Tac-Toe

Draw a line through the pictures that start with the same letter.

A B C D E F G H I J K L M N O P Q R S T U V W X Y Z

How Many?

Find the pictures that start with the letters **s**, **t**, and **u**.

Beginning Sounds

Say the picture words. Circle the letters that begin the picture words.

S
T
U

S
T
U

Letter Match

Draw lines from the uppercase letters to the matching lowercase letters.

S

T   t

U   u

             s

S
T
U

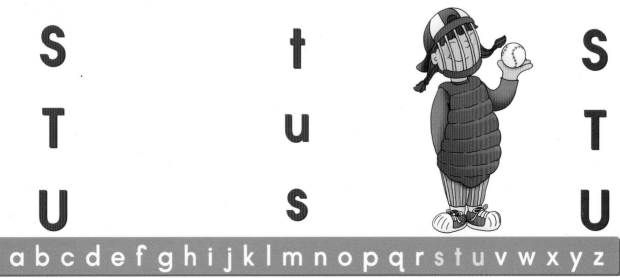

a b c d e f g h i j k l m n o p q r s t u v w x y z

Practice tracing and writing each letter.

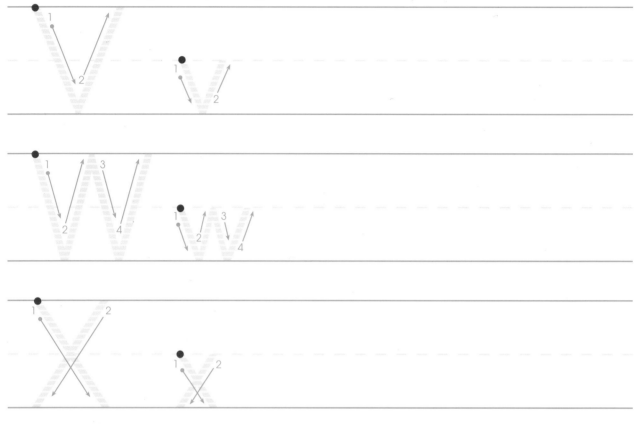

Beginning Sounds

Write the letters that begin the picture words.

_____ ase

_____ orm

_____ -ray

Tic-Tac-Toe

Draw a line through the pictures that start with the same letter.

A B C D E F G H I J K L M N O P Q R S T U V W X Y Z

How Many?

Find the pictures that start with the letters **v**, **w**, and **x**.

Beginning Sounds

Say the picture words. Circle the letters that begin the picture words.

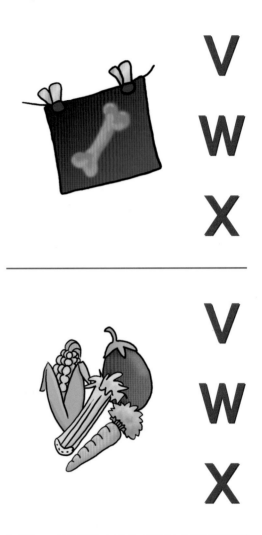

V

W

X

V

W

X

Letter Match

Draw lines from the uppercase letters to the matching lowercase letters.

V   x

W   v

X   w

V

W

X

a b c d e f g h i j k l m n o p q r s t u v w x y z

Alphabet Fun!

Practice tracing and writing each letter.

Letter Match

Draw lines from the uppercase letters to the matching lowercase letters.

Y   z

Z   y

Beginning Sounds

Write the letters that begin the picture words.

_____ arn

_____ ipper

Tic-Tac-Toe

Draw a line through the pictures that start with the same letter.

A B C D E F G H I J K L M N O P Q R S T U V W X Y Z

abcdefghijklmnopqrstuvwxyz

BEGINNING SOUNDS: R, F, P, C, H, M

Say each picture word.
Write each beginning sound.
Use these letters: **r**, **f**, **p**, **c**, **h**, **m**.

_____ ie

_____ an

_____ ain

_____ at

_____ at

_____ an

_____

a b c d e f g h i j k l m n o p q r s t u v w x y z

BEGINNING SOUNDS: K, T, L, B, Q, D

Say each picture word.
Write each beginning sound.
Use these letters: **k**, **t**, **l**, **b**, **q**, **d**.

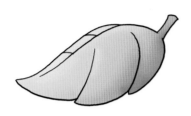

___ eaf

___ ie

___ ueen

___ og

___ ite

___ all

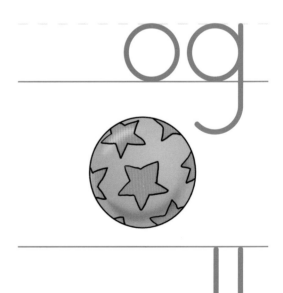

a b c d e f g h i j k l m n o p q r s t u v w x y z

Alphabet Fun!

Say each picture word.
Write each ending sound.
Use these letters: **m**, **k**, **d**, **l**, **f**, **r**.

dru

sea

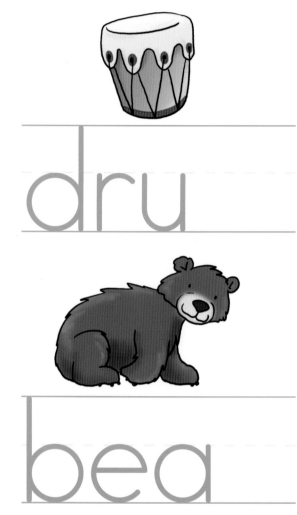

bea

be

boo

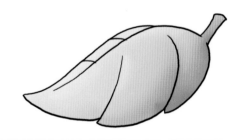

lea

a b c d e f g h i j k l m n o p q r s t u v w x y z

ENDING SOUNDS: B, G, L, N, P, X

Say each picture word.
Write each ending sound.
Use these letters: **b, g, l, n, p, x**.

pi_____

we_____

cu_____

ow_____

su_____

fo_____

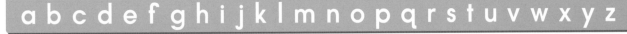

a b c d e f g h i j k l m n o p q r s t u v w x y z

Alphabet Fun!

ALPHABETICAL ORDER

Write the letters in order from A to Z.

A B C D E F G H I J K L M N O P Q R S T U V W X Y Z

Alphabet Fun!

Alphabet Fun!

IT'S A MIX-UP!

Read the four letters in each row.
Write the letters in order below.
The first row is done for you.

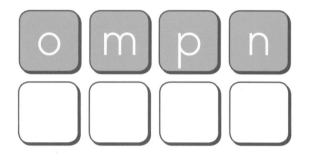

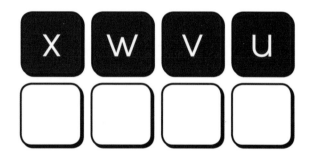

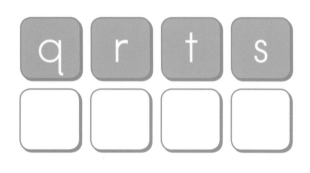

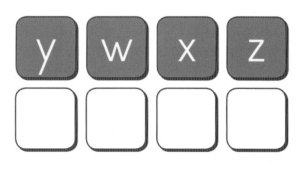

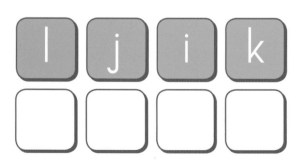

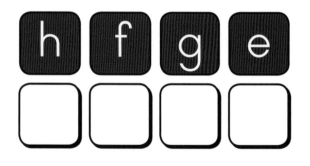

a b c d e f g h i j k l m n o p q r s t u v w x y z

Alphabet Fun!